I0163917

Putting God Given Thoughts & Wonders on the Mind & Heart with Something to Think About

Copyright ©2015 by Alice Castle

All rights reserved. No part of this book may be produced in any form without written permission from Acute Xpressions.

Printed in the U.S.A.

*All scripture quotations are from the New King James Version of the Bible.

Acute Xpressions®

Putting God Given Thoughts

& Wonders on the

Mind & Heart with

Something to Think About

Alice Castle

This book is dedicated to my mom, my dad, and my children who all have inspired and helped me through the years to work gracefully and acknowledge God; the almighty in our lives.

Wisdom is that which enables men to judge what is the best means of attaining them. Prudence is practical wisdom applied in the best time and manner to secure the best ends.

In giving honor to God, who is first in my life and to Jim. These two men have stuck closer to me than anyone else. When my friends were too busy, God and Jim was there through the storms and rains in my life. Jim is the best thing; he means a lot to me and I would not trade him for Nothing. I could not have done this alone.

"Jim is <u>Jesus</u> <u>In</u> <u>Me</u>"

Good Morning,

This is GOD! I will be handling all your problems today.
I will <u>not</u> need your help ~

So, have a good day.

To my mom and dad who raised me up the right way and to do the right thing. Sometimes I felt like I could just run away but I'm glad I didn't because what I know now, I am so glad I didn't. It also helped me to realize that being home was more honorable than ever.

Life is not what you think in your mind when you're a child and you don't really know any better until you grow up and learn more.

My dad, Reverend Wilmer Castle and mom Lucille Castle told me something one day and it stuck with me all through my life until now and it's still there. They said:

"The <u>will</u> is the <u>power</u> by which the <u>mind</u> accepts a <u>thought</u> <u>strong</u> <u>enough</u> that it must <u>carry</u> it <u>out</u>."

My children inspired me too and they were with me all the way. My daughter "Shantell" said, "mom I know it will be alright because God said through him all things are possible and I know you got God with you and all around you".

My oldest son "Shelby" told me, "hey! Girl keep looking to Jim. He brought you this far and he can take you farther because you have walked through the valley and the shadow of death. I know with him, you have No Fear".

My baby boy "Jermaine" said, I know the Lord will make a way because you can't walk alone because you have Jim with you. I know with him, that Grace and Mercy covers you. Plus all of us have seen Jim work things out for you".

God's blessings are all around us. All we have to do is Believe and Receive it. I hope by reading this book, it will open a door for you or someone in your life. Get God, Get Jim, and with the two of them, you will have a full committed life and the right ones on your team.

The Team Committee

| Grace | Love | Joy | Hope |
| Mercy | Peace | Favor | Patience |

"You won't know where you are going, until you know where you came from"

Traveling down a road that never ends.

But with the help of the team committee, you will make it.

Father I come before you right now in Jesus name and declare that every curse that has come on me and my family and my finances in every way by the words that I have spoken is broken and reverses in Jesus name from this moment on. And, father, I prophesy that my family and I will serve God. That prosperity is mine and my family. Salvation is mine and my family, Deliverance is mine and my family, Healing is mine and my family, I claim it and speak it into existence in Jesus name.

Everything I put my hands on, God will cause it to prosper.

As for me and my family we shall prosper and be saved.

I cancel every negative word spoken.

I fully expect God to open doors that have been shut and every negative thing spoken against me to be broken and reversed. I speak spiritual restoration greater than before all in Jesus name.

God's Grace, Mercy, Favor, Peace & Joy

But the greatest is "Love"

Faith

Brings Strength and Hope

"Grace"

I lost my home by fire because of the man I lived with got mad and burned down my home and everything I had. All was left was the clothes on my back and all my kids had were the clothes on their back. But with God and the faith I had, I knew his Grace and Favor would cover me and my kids.

Grace -- -- -- Free and Undeserved Love and Favor of God toward man as a sinner. The grace of God is unmerited. It is a gift to those who will receive. All you have to do is receive the gift and unwrap it. Think of it as a present.

Receive grace when you ask him to come in your life. You give "mercy" it is compassion and pity; and it is the same as the right thing to do.

God's

Grace – he spoke

Mercy – he gave

Peace – he lived

Not of men; neither by men; but by Jesus Christ.

Grace – Ephesians 4:7, 2 Corinthians 9:8, 12:9

Drop the G

Race – Run the Race with Grace

Drop the R

Ace – You have an Ace in your pocket as you run the race with Grace.

Revelation.1:8, 11 21:6   22:13

ACE >> Aint Christ Enough

He is <u>A</u>ccurate

<u>C</u>ertified

<u>E</u>ffective

2 Corinthians 12:9

But he said to me, "My grace is sufficient for you, for my power is made perfect in weakness." Therefore I will boast all the more gladly about my weaknesses, so that Christ's power may rest on me.

Romans 8:28

And we know that in all things God works for the good of those who love him, who[a] have been called according to his purpose.

Although I was going through a great loss, God was there to assure me that I had not lost anything because I had him and Jim who can replace anything lost or needed.

The 2

Let's look at a "sandwich". You have 2 slices of bread; one is grace (the top slice) and the other is mercy (the bottom slice) and everything else is in the middle. But as long as it is covered with the right covering, all things will work out. It will taste just like God want it to! But knowing we are covered with Grace and Mercy brings us joy to the heart and a smile on the face.

His grace is receiving him knowing him and finding his will in your life. Then ask him to do it, thank him for doing it, and go your way rejoicing that the victory is already won through his grace.

In your spare time, study the book of Philemon 1st chapter.

There are 3 instances we need to look as to why people come into our lives.

> For a Reason --- Moses, Elijah
> For a Season --- Moses, Philemon 1:15
> For to Stay --- God, Holy Ghost

Realize why God sent them and pray.

Receive it only for awhile

Know that God had something to do with all of them and let it stay on your heart and minds that it is God's will for you.

The Reason...

To help or show you something that is needed to be acknowledged. Moses was led by God to lead the children of Israel out of the wilderness and that was his reason for being placed in Pharaoh's house.

The Season...

Is only for a certain length of time. You prepare for each season. Some things only come for a while and then they're gone. Keep God with you at all times and his word hidden in your heart. His love and forgiveness is forever.

When certain persons come into your life, you need to know the difference and the reason for them being there. Some persons come only to help you to learn a specific thing. Those are the ones who are there for a season. Pray and ask God to show you the difference.

"Thought for the Day"

Knowledge is knowing and obtaining information through study and experience. Wisdom is understanding how to use it.

To Stay…

Means to remain or to be there permanently; never to leave. To stay by your side through it all. God is the answer and he is always there even when you feel like he isn't.

There was a time in my life when I felt empty and lost. But, when I think about where God has brought me from and what he has done for me, all I could do is throw my hands up and say "Lord, I love you. Don't ever leave me. My mind, heart, body, and soul are all yours. You are my everlasting friend, buddy; ace coon boom".

"Days of Our Lives"

Thank God for the wisdom of looking up to him and not looking down. For you know, you will not be able to see yesterday anymore. But you thank God for seeing today and that he blesses you to see tomorrow. Remember God is the only one for all your blessed days.

~ Ms. Good Time Alice

A Note for You…

Proverbs 3:5-6

Trust in the Lord with all your heart and lean not on your own understanding; in all your ways submit to him, and he will make your paths straight.

The 9 Washing Powders of Life

A while back when I was going through some things in life as we all do at some point in our lives, the word of God told me to get up and go the store. To share this story with you is a blessing. Well anyway, I had this puzzled look on my face and asked myself, "Why would I go to the store when I don't have anything to get"? Not to mention I didn't have any money and nothing to buy. So the Holy Spirit kept at it trying to convince me to go to the store and eventually I picked up my keys and went to the store.

Low and behold, as I was just walking around the store, the Lord spoke to me telling me to go to the detergent aisle. As I began to look, the Lord told me look at the different kinds of laundry detergent. This is what he revealed to me:

Tide...

He took me to Galatians 6:9 and Thessalonians 3:13. Be not weary in well doing, for in due season, we shall reap if we faint not. Don't get tired of doing good, just keep on pushing. There is goodness to reap so we must endure. The Tide washing powder reminded me of becoming tired or weary. Using God word can clean out the wrong thoughts and we won't become weary with the weight of thinking the wrong things.

Cheer... John 16:33

I was so excited I had to hurry up and get the paper and pencil to write it down because God was using me. So now its "cheer up Alice, it's all good". John 16:33 says be of good cheer because as we go through life, we will have tribulation, but still be of good cheer. I have overcome the world because Jim was and still is with me. You can do it, just believe and be of good cheer.

Stop Thinking about How Big Your problem is

And

Start Telling Your Problem How Big Your

GOD

Is

When You're Down to Nothing

God is up to Something

The Faithful See the Invisible

Believe the Incredible

And Then Receive the Impossible

Every <u>Action</u> You Take is A Seed You

Sow, And Every Seed You Sow is A Harvest

You'll Reap

Gain... Matthew 16:26

For what is a man profited, if he shall gain the whole world and lose his own soul? Or, what shall a man give in exchange for his soul? Now, I began to let my mind ponder on God more as he gave me this word. Don't ever lose the Lord because no matter what you have, it came from him and through him. He helped you get this far and will surely take you even farther.

You can't take things with you when you die so be sure not to make things your life. The world did not give it and the world cannot take it away. But, you can have God all through life and live with him in Heaven.

All... Proverb 3:6, Matthew 11:28

In all thy ways acknowledge him and he shall direct thy paths. I can do all things through Christ which strengthen me... Philippians 4:13

Even though you are heavy laden and labor hard; going through all types of situations in life, he tell us in Matthew 11:28 "Come unto me all ye who labor and are heavy laden and I will give you rest. He can take out the trash if you allow him to come in and clean you up. He shall supply all your needs according to his riches and glory by Christ Jesus. Philippians 4:19

I know this message is for someone who may be reading this. All of the washing powders are useful so use the powder God has for you and be clean and stay washed up. It does not matter what kind you use because they all have God's power in them.

If God Brings
Me To It

He Will Bring
Me Through It

By this time, the people in the store thought I was crazy after seeing me have this fellowship with the washing powders. Some of the employees who were observing me even thought I was trying to steal something but I explained to them how God was using me. They were amazed as I witnessed to them and some even began to cry and confess to me how their lives were a mess and needed to be cleaned up. They began to tell me how I had blessed them through this episode. You never know what God has for you until you try and do what he wants you to do.

Fab... 1 Timothy 1:4
Don't give heed to fables and endless genealogies. Drop the les and you have Fab. Sometimes we can overlook or miss what God's trying to tell us through his word. We may have to dissect some of the scripture to fully grasp the meaning to what we're reading in the bible. Fable means misconception, error, or mistake. We have all been deceived at one point or another and we tend to make mistakes from time to time. Study the word right and do the

right thing. Sometimes what we say can be received the wrong way.

Paul, the apostle of Jesus Christ, was liberated from prison and he went into Macedonia preaching and teaching God's word. He told Timothy not to teach any other doctrine except the one God gave them. There were teachers who were constantly seeking to bring Christians back under the Law of Moses. Anything that is delivered by word of mouth as a legendary tale as opposed to a historical account is a Fable; foolish or improbable story. Be mindful of what you're receiving as well as what you're releasing.

Surf...2 Corinthians 12:9

My Grace is sufficient for thee; for my strength is made perfect in weakness. When I think of surf, I think of riding the waves at the waves. But here it's God's sufficient grace. Oftentimes, the rides in life are rough but God assured Paul that his sufficient grace is to provide all things and that we should learn to depend wholly upon the power of God. Receive him, believe in him, look to him and keep him at all times.

Wisk... Proverbs 4:7

Wisdom is like the secret to life and health to all who obey. Wisdom is the principle thing; therefore get wisdom and understanding. Solomon asked for wisdom which is greatest of all riches or fame he had. We need wisdom to help us through everyday life and to make right decisions. Exalt wisdom and it will promote you to do well. Wisdom will help put the right thoughts in our minds.

No Matter What Happens...

No Matter How Bad Things Get...

No Matter What is Taken From You...

Nobody Can Ever Take Away Your Faith...

Purex…Matthew 5:8

Blessed are the pure in heart, for they shall see God. This is a new birth; pure and clean. We need to keep ourselves clean on the inside as well as the outside. Bad thoughts and other bad stuff get inside us and we hinder ourselves from allowing God to use us for his glory. We need to keep his word inside of us and keep out the trash.

Era...95:10

Forty years long was I grieved with this generation, and said, it is a people that do err in their heart, and they have not known my ways. We err in heart because we tend to listen to the mind instead of the heart. Proverbs 14:22

says Do they not err that devise evil? But mercy and truth shall be to them that devise good. Lies and hate causes us to err in life and make bad decisions.

My Father's House

"I will rise and go"

The Lost Son

"Where are you going?"

"Are you there yet?"

"Do you know where you are going?"

You may want it now but God says not yet. By the time it all comes together, it's in longer, it's right there in front of you.

Put the right things in your mind because the mind is a terrible thing to waste. Think on scripture of God's word. A son left home but had to return as a result of his fall. He thought the money he possessed would last forever. But money is not everything. Love covered it all.

Luke 15:18 I will arise and go to my father, and will say unto him, Father, I have sinned against heaven, and before thee.

God gave me this thought on the scripture that said: You had me, (his father) you left me, and now you want to come back. There is a saying; you never miss your water until your well runs dry. Or, you never miss your baby until she bid you goodbye.

We think we got it good but eventually it all falls to pieces. If God is not in the equation, then nothing good will come from it. We get nervous and upset, can't handle and want to run away from it. But the answer is not in our running. We need to face our giants and work on it with faith until God sees us through. When we go to the father, he can see what no one else sees. This is why we should rejoice when one comes to God.

Romans 3:23 For all have sinned, and come short of the glory of God. The son told his father he had sinned. The father did not see the sin but instead he saw his son with a bleeding soul crying out for love and help. He looked beyond the fault and saw a need.

Isaiah 1:18 Come now, and let us reason together, saith the Lord: though your sins be as scarlet, they shall be white as snow; though they be red like crimson, they shall be as wool.

Don't leave God

The son left home and sometimes we leave God thinking it's alright. When things get bad and out of place, we try and go back to fix it. The son had a home but he chose to leave. He and his father had what we call that come back kind of love because his father welcomed him back with open arms. God forgives us because of the love he has for us. Hs grace, love and mercy cover us. God also has that come back kind of love towards us, his children.

'The Woman God Wants me to Be'

W - - the wonderful word of wisdom that lives inside of her. Proverb 31:26

O - - is obedient in growing old in the word, not in the world. Psalm 16:11

M - - is the mighty strength she has Proverb 31:17&25

A - - the amazing things she does. Proverb 31:10-28

N - - is for the noble life she lives. Proverb 31:30

'The Man God wants me to Be'

The M&M Man

'He will stand for something and fall for nothing'

M - - is for the mighty man and master that lives inside of me. Proverb 16:16

A - - is for the good attitude from wisdom and knowledge; understanding what to do. Proverb 20:7

N - - is for the nature of God in him. Genesis 2:7

There is a movie called "Are you there yet". Now ask yourself "Are you there yet", where God needs you to be? If not, you should get on the right road; arise and return to what you abandoned for the enemy. Sometimes we go in circles, but the good news is that God will make a way for us to escape. Then there will be a homecoming we'll never forget once we allow God to come in.

Don't miss your homecoming, go home to God! He has a great meal for each of us and everyone in our family. Don't worry, he's got our back, front, side, top and bottom.

No weapon formed against you shall prosper,
And every tongue which rises against you in judgment
You shall condemn.
This is the heritage of the servants of the LORD,
And their righteousness is from Me,"
Says the LORD.

Isaiah 54:17

The Fisherman

In this lesson, we talk about Peter by the boat. In the book of John 21:15-16, God says to feed his lamb and his sheep. In Luke 5:1-6, remember when you do as God says, the impossible become possible. Listen, learn and lead a good life. We are all fishers of men.

When you don't have anything and no one to talk to, try Jesus. He should be first!

My parents taught me to fish when I was young so when my boys were old enough, I took them fishing too. I remember my youngest son Corwin preparing his reel but then he did something strange. He tied a string around his foot and threw the line into the water. I asked him what he did that for. He said, "Mom, I want to know how much strength a fish has when he pulls on the line." Then I asked him, "What does that have to do with fishing?" His reply was, "I know that life can pull at different strengths depending on the size of the problem. What is your strength in God? What are you fishing with? Grace, mercy, or is the devil pulling you?

As we go through life sharing and witnessing to others the good news, we need the right tools. Fishing can be compared to how we deal with different types of people (the fish). There are different approaches needed to reach different individuals and we need to use different bait. Study to show yourself approved.

6 Things Needed to go Fishing

Rod	Hook	Reel
Line	Bait	Net

1. The rod is the "Word". (Bible)....

If you have a bible, use it and don't just let it collect dust somewhere. It is like a gun with no bullets if you don't load it and use it. ***Psalm 119:11 says, Your word I have hidden*** *in my heart,*

That I might not sin against You.

> *Psalm 119:105 says, Your word is a lamp to my feet And a light to my path.*

Watch It, Know What,

How and When to use the word…

2. The Line is "Prayer"…

1Thessalonians 5:17 says Pray without ceasing.

James 5:16 says The effective, fervent prayer of a righteous man avails much. My mom use to tell me that prayer is the key and faith unlocks the door. So keep smiling while you are praying and use your faith to open up doors. How? Work on it. (Smile)

3. The hook is "faith" ….

There are all kinds of hooks but only one kind of faith to hook the problem or situation you are going through. That is the faith in God. *Matthew 17:20 say if you have faith as a mustard seed, you will say to this mountain, 'Move from here to there,' and it will move; and nothing will be impossible for you.*

Hebrews 11:6; But without faith it is impossible to please Him, for he who comes to God must believe that He is, and that He is a rewarder of those who diligently seek Him.

4.   The bait is "Love"....

John 15:12; This is My commandment, that you love one another as I have loved you.

Romans 13:10; Love does no harm to a neighbor; therefore love is the fulfillment of the law.

1 Corinthians 13:13; And now abide faith, hope, love, these three; but the greatest of these is love. Bait comes in different forms, shapes and sizes. Some people worm their way into your life. But no matter what, use the real deal, love the right way.

5.   The reel is "common sense"....

We have to turn the reel to bring the fish in so as we study the word, pray with faith, and show love, we'll reel in a catch. Someone will see this in us and began to come to Christ and/or have a thought of how he/she must be saved. Use common sense along with wisdom.

Jeremiah 49:7; Against Edom.

Thus says the LORD of hosts:

"*Is* wisdom no more in Teman?
Has counsel perished from the prudent?
Has their wisdom vanished?

The question is, where is the common sense and the wisdom? They both go together.

6.   The net is the "Church"…

In Luke 5:2-11, Simon Peter begin to hear the word of God and he believed and had faith. Through prayer, his love challenged him to cast his net and it allowed him to make the catch of a lifetime. Listening and obeying the right way leads to a big catch. In order to get a great catch, we need to fish with the right bait. It will increase the church body and we wouldn't have room to receive. Not to mention the place of worship would enlarge and we would need to expand to accommodate everyone. Feed a man a fish for one day and he will only eat for that day but teach a man to fish and he will eat for a lifetime. Don't just use the word for one day, but acknowledge and use it for a lifetime.

The word is precious and we can understand the knowledge and wisdom God gives us.

The Want Ad

Help Wanted: Workers needed on the inside. *Hebrew 12:1, Wherefore seeing we also are compassed about with so great a cloud of witnesses, let us lay aside every weight, and the sin which doth so easily beset us, and let us run with patience the race that is set before us.*

If we scrape a knee or cut a finger, nip a toe nail or crack a bone, pain or hurt follows. We can apply a Band-Aid or rub medicine, but the hurt inside takes a different toll. We have to allow God to come in to do the work that is needed. Greater is he who is in me than he who is in the world. To allow him in means to allows his words to range in us. His words are like medicine to the marrow of the bones.

I thought this day would never come, but I just filed for a divorce. Divorcing my past, divorcing my pain, divorcing my doubt, divorcing my negativity, divorcing my haters, my setbacks, and divorcing what I lack. The judge gave me full custody of my call, full custody of my life. Divorce yourself from your past, so your future can be released!

Take the Trash Out

We take trash out of our homes because we don't want the place to stink and we don't want our environment to be messy and dirty. The same should be the standard for our lives.

There are situations, circumstances and people that enter our lives just as the trash enters our homes. Like our homes we need to rid our lives of the situations and people that bring on the mess. People can pollute your life. They can bring on situations and circumstances that bring stress in your life. None of these things are profitable to the kingdom and they need to be addressed. If not, they will control you and won't have a life. You'll be subjected to their whims and desires.

Make a move to take the trash out of your life and live a life that's more free...more fun, has a better fragrance and allows you to do the things God would have you to do. If you don't know what that is, perhaps once you clear the trash, you'll be better able to hear him.

Be encouraged, inspired and motivated to move!

The Lord will give strength unto his people; the
Lord will bless his people with peace.

Thought for the Week

I can do all things through Christ who strengthens me
Philippians 4:13

The road to success is not straight. There is a curve called failure, a loop called confusion, speed bumps called friends, red lights called enemies, and caution lights called family. We will have flats called jobs. But, if we have a spare called determination, an engine called perseverance, insurance called faith, a driver called Jesus, we will make to a place called success.

Faith

Faith is

F – Is Forsaking

A – Is All

I – Issues and

T – Taking it to

H – Him "God", Jesus in your life.

The greatest abundance we may ask or even think, according to the power that works in us. [Ephesians 3:20]. 2 Peter 1:5-7

His ability is connected with his willingness to do for his people. There are no limitations in getting things from God according to the promises in 2 Peter 1:3-5.

The joy of having a powerful friendship with a man such as God is so great. He's a friend who you can call at anytime. He covers us at all times with his grace and mercy. The power is the connection that the two of us have together. Where is your power coming from? Are you connected to the right source? What kind of friendship do you have?

The man I loved and cherished so much hurt me unbelievably. He hurt me so much and one day he decided to burn down our home. The only clothing I had was the clothes on my back and the same for my kids.

I lived after that and I had to let it go; forgive and forget. Forgiving him was hard but God and Jim brought me through it. After losing my home, I lived with my parents for a while but sooner than later, I had to leave. I was hurting inside out and just could not find any peace. I later decided to move to Baton Rouge and as I was packing, I cried and the tears would not stop. The tears continued uncontrollably as I was getting into the car preparing for my journey. I had nothing to look forward to and nothing to look back on except hurt and pain. As I was driving across the big, long bridge, I contemplated getting out of my car and jumping off into the river but a small voice said to me "if you jump, your problem still won't be solved." I said between tears, I don't have anything anyway, and the voice replied, "You have me"

I said who, Jim? Who, what is that as I looked around and didn't see anyone. Then my mind shifted back to jumping off that bridge and that voice continued to vex me. I heard the words "I love you" and "I'm Jim" He said experience is a hard teacher. The test comes first but in the end there is a lesson to be learned so the results can be greater.

After that little conversation with Jim, I changed my mind about jumping because it was at that moment; I realized God had something for me to do. I asked God to please guide my feet while I walk and run this race. I needed him more than ever. So the voice spoke to me again and told me that I was not alone.

Since then, Jim and I have been together for thirty years and it's such a blessing to know I have someone I can depend on at all times. I've been delighted to share with others about my friend Jim. I had to forgive and let go of the hurt inside and out to allow God to come in and do a work in me. So I got it together and kept looking up to God and Jim with a smile. I became the happy woman I am today. People ask me how I can be so happy and joyous all the time. They say to me I act as if nothing ever goes on in my life that brings me stress. But they only see the outside. I'm covered by Jim inside and out. I'm equipped with the word of God to reach out to others. God needs us to have eyes that see, not just look. Eyes that look is common but it's rare to find eyes that actually see. Don't just look at the outside of others but see what's on the inside.

Humpty Dumpty sat on the wall. Humpty Dumpty had a great fall. All the king's horses and all the king's men could not put Humpty back together again.

Micah 7:8, Rejoice not against me, O mine enemy: when I fall, I shall arise; when I sit in darkness, the Lord shall be a light unto me.

Psalm 37:24, Though he fall, he shall not be utterly cast down: for the Lord upholdeth him with his hand.

A little talk to the enemy is all we need. We have to face the devil and not talk behind his back. The devil loves backbiting and talking about folks.

Don't look at me and say "girl that's good for her" or she must have done something wrong. When I fall, I'll have a little talk alright but not too long with the devil. But a little talk with Jesus will make it right. The enemy will try and talk to offer things but be ye strong and steadfast, unmovable and always abounding in the word of the Lord. For we shall arise. For the Lord upholds me with his hand.

Jeremiah 30:17, For I will restore health unto thee, and I will heal thee of thy wounds, saith the Lord; because they called thee an Outcast, saying, This is Zion, whom no man seeketh after.

Isaiah 1:18, Come now, and let us reason together, saith the Lord.

Jerusalem was to be rebuilt like Humpty Dumpty but you see they could not put him back but thanks be to God the almighty. The potter wants to put the pieces back together again. There are some spots that need to be worked on and only God's power can make it right.

After all that I've been through and all the hurt James caused me, he came to me one day and asked for my help. I helped him because I had God on the inside of me. Later I found out that he had been diagnosed with cancer and he died. God said it was his time to go and told me not to worry. I helped him when he needed me the most and God assured me that I had done what many would not have done in my situation.

So I share with you for you to just be mindful of how you treat others because you never know when you may need help from the very person who you stepped on and mistreated.

Don't Put God in the Freezer

Either we're cold or we're hot but we can't be both. If we're lukewarm, he'll spit us out! I used to work, work, work and then come home and take care of my mother, cook for my three kids and make sure all my house work was completed by eleven thirty or twelve o'clock at night. The only time I would pick up my bible was on Sunday when I went to church. One day all that changed after I passed out from working so hard and allowing stress to take over my life. My son had to rush me to the hospital and the doctor told me that I was overworked and stressed out.

It was at that moment, I knew I had to do something and I needed help from God to do it. God was my only way out! I had placed God in the freezer but it was at this point, I needed to take him out. We place God in the freezer all the time; place him on the back burner until we really think we need him. I realized I needed God first thing in the morning and all throughout the day and night to help me on this journey.

I began to read my bible day in and day out; every chance I got. I did not just read but I studied the words I was reading and I allowed those words to minister to my heart. I had to take God out of the freezer once and for all. He then began to work with me and gave me the insight I needed to produce this book.

Don't place God in the freezer and take him out when you believe you need him to do something for you or in your life. We may never get a chance to take him out once we put him away.

"Guard your thoughts because they may become your words. Guard your words because they may become your actions. Guard your actions because they may become your character. And guard your character because it determines your destiny!"

Your Registration Sticker

If your spiritual life had to be inspected like a car, how would you rate it?

Registration and License -------

Many people claim to be Christians but when examined in the light of God's word, they really have no authority to operate under the name of Christians.

In order to get your license:

John 1:12 ~ But as many as received him, to them gave he power to become the sons of God, even to them that believe on his name.

John 14:6 ~ Jesus saith unto him, I am the way, the truth, and the life: no man cometh unto the Father, but by me.

Act 4:12 ~ Neither is there salvation in any other: for there is none other name under heaven given among men, whereby we must be saved.

Romans 3:26 ~ To declare, I say, at this time his righteousness: that he might be just, and the justifier of him which believeth in Jesus.

Galatians 3:26 ~ For ye are all the children of God by faith in Christ Jesus.

"Do all the good you can,

By all the means you can,

In all the ways you can,

In all the places you can,

At all the times you can,

To all the people you can,

As long as ever you can."

Kindness means more than

You'll ever guess because

With God all things are possible

Matthew 19:26

You are precious in my sight

Isaiah 43:4

"The Lord's blessings are before you, behind you, and around you, to remind you, you are treasured, you are precious and you are loved."

"ASK"   **"SEEK"**   **"KNOCK"**

Luke 18:1   Jeremiah 29:13   Luke 11:10

ASSURANCE   SECURITY   KEEPER OR KEY

To *ask* *i*mplies *want*; seeking implies *loss* and knocking implies *need*. One must *ask* with confidence and humility; *seek* with care and application, and *knock* with earnestness and perseverance.

If there is doubt; it is because of the failure to *ask in faith*; Isaiah 5:8; Nothing wavering; to *seek* diligently and to *knock* with importunity. The only reason for unanswered prayer (Luke 11:5-13 ~ 18:1-8) to a Christian is *"unbelief"* (Matthew 17:17-21; James 1:5-8)

{ 3 Fold Assurance of an Answer}

"Receive"   **"Findeth"**   **"It Shall Be Open"**

"Faith is the *fuel* that allows people to *obtain common* and *uncommon* results" *Faith* is born from the seed of the word (1Peter 1:23) Faith grows as it *feeds* on the *word* (1Peter 2:2) Faith without works is dead. Jesus told Peter to step out of the boat and walk on the water. The word was spoken, *but faith was born only after Peter stepped out.* (Matthew 14:28-29)

The source of *faith* is the *word*.

The substance of *faith* is *action*.

Hi Ladies, Hi Men What's Up?
This is From "<u>Capital One</u>"

The both of you really need to read this letter and pay close attention to what the spirit has to say, to the church. Where is "Jim" in this world? Now think about that for a moment! If I have a strong church life and all the education of this life, what's the problem or where is the problem? What really matters in this life?

The most important things come from my renewed mind, from the spiritual mind of Christ Jesus. All of us have the light of the world. Ain't no devil in hell can stop you and since the enemy is at work, you should be at work too in the kingdom of God. Don't allow the devil to get you down, put him down under your feet and walk high. What's wrong?

A spiritual giant can handle any demon, any kind of attack; night or day! It's good to have a conversation face to face because on paper and over just isn't enough. Call on your "Helper"! That's what he sent Jesus and Jim for; the Holy Spirit is not in the church. It's inside of you. "Call" on your helper and please find out how to use the power. Open doors, open up windows, open up a business, handle diversity, line different people up in line, etc….. Nothing can stand against the solid foundation of Christ".

Let your helper operate in you every day of your life activities. The truth will set you free from all daily problems.

Everything obeys what has power over it, to control it, to happen in a certain way. It will not lay down on you. Use what you got to get what you need. Have confidence in yourself. Power is a force controlled by you. Just direct it in your favor. Nothing is lost; it's just waiting on you to do something with it. What's on paper is used to speak out of your mouth.

Action comes from the information you already have; faith moves everything so use it. Pride and confidence walk together but confidence holds you up when pride fails. Please understand it's an honor and a privilege just to be able to talk and share this word that God has given to me. I love everyone from my heart. All things have to deal with God because it has to follow the order of his plans. Put everything on one table and take a good look at it. Let the paperwork say something to you. Then put everything on one accord. Lift it up and what stays up, keep it up. Whatever falls, stand on it for a new foundation. Whatever you set up or have for your business, that's what you do. Read what you are dealing with.

Don't change to please anything or anyone. People will come and go so let go and this will leave room for the right kind of people to come into your life. Take out the bad to get the good in. Just do your thing and don't worry about the rest. Use what you have learned from the past and your helper will help you put it together. Your work in this life is what has full power over. It works for you; just tell it what to do. Don't let it tell you!

Remember knowledge is the plan. Wisdom is putting the plan together and understanding is on how to use it.

"Capital One, Over and Out"

The battle is not yours, But God
2 Chronicles 20:15-17

L ife is a journey and a destination with all types of battles. But the battle is not yours, its Gods'. At the end of each life is a legacy of love. God is love and God's gift of faith, time, and memory helps us to gather the love that is behind us; the love that is now and the love before us. A sunset on earth is a sunrise in heaven for someone. The precious love of God is that one will be remembered forever because God fought the battle for you and me.

As I began to go through different situations in my life, I looked around and my tears could not even come out. The hurt was so bad but eventually I had to force it out some kind of way. There was nothing for me to cling to and no one to talk to. BUT ONE MAN. I could not sleep so I thought about a man named "Jim" and I said "you know what, I need him because I can call him anytime in the morning and late in the midnight hours. He is Just, Effective, Unique, and Sweet. The only one who can bring me through whatever I'm dealing with. I said to myself, I need him with me, in me, and all around me at all times. So I called him Jim; the man of all qualities without any question. The Jesus in me. So to keep a good thing, hold on to it and never ever let go of "Jim".

www.ingramcontent.com/pod-product-compliance
Lightning Source LLC
Chambersburg PA
CBHW020520030426
42337CB00011B/483